LOVING ACROSS GALAXIES

This is for the man who showed me what it is to be loved. This is for the one who showed me what sharing a life, even from a distance, was like. This is for the man who showed me that love can be unspoken, through the eyes, and the hours of silence spent on a call. This is for the one who showed me how all the little things equal love.

This is for Marcus.

This is for me.

This is for us.

LOVING ACROSS GALAXIES

ALEXANDRIA GREEN

Contents

Before Him...

Special Place

They said I was too different to be loved...

* * *

"Hell is a special place for people like you."
And the criteria to be "like me" is: ungrateful.
like an adorable raccoon in the trash—
"That's where you belong, did you know that?"
—unkind, as a parakeet furiously biting at skin, refusing to
 be near a soul; maybe they just need some alone time.
Lastly, uncontrollable, like a golden retriever with its favorite
 bone.
"Satan is in this one."
Hell is for people like us—human, independent, and free.
Someone who wants to be loved unconditionally.
Someone who will not bend.
Someone who is breaking.

I Am Not Your Wonder Woman

I love wearing cowl tops that curve to my breasts and expose
my midriff.
The way they make me feel is the most important thing to
me: powerful, sexy, confident.
I am my own Wonder Woman in those tops, carrying a shield
and sword as I take to a dance floor.
I swish my hips like it is my personal battlefield and I will
conquer

not be conquered, I say to you.
I did not wear my sword and shield so that you could traipse
across my battlefield as if you owned it!
An unwanted trespasser among the heavy beat of the war
music
telling me that I wore this top to be noticed.

I came to conquer, I say. To make the music and the field of
   battle submit
to my will and my will alone,
A woman who can stand among men of steel and a god of
   speed
not a man who plays like he can win no matter how hard I
   say no, no matter how hard I swing my sword and shield.

Not even when I tell him to go find somewhere else to stick
   it; some other field of battle,
since the only sword I will touch is my own
and the only thing that will touch my hips as I defeat this
   beat is air, is sweat.
I am not your Wonder Woman, I am *my* own Wonder
   Woman.

Empty and Too Much

Do I feel anything but
A bottomless black pit of nothingness.
A deep broken trench in the ocean,
without a light—nothing
but a blackened emptiness.

Other times—too much
My whole body—my whole soul—a raging fire!
An escapable, cataclysmic heat!
A dark roaring, stormy night, with drowning rainfire
It never ceases!

Let the sky shine bright and wondrously!
again. I know it won't.

The Old Language

Centuries of Tears
churning—boiling—roaring—inside of me.
burning me.
breaking and crashing in me.
They ebb and They flow
and They burst!
Inside.
Inside of me—
stop!
Trespass no longer!

Algae and Achlys,
your creators, your saviors
My locked doors were nothing to them.
My insides—my Heart—my Soul bent and wept
because of them.
You tormentors!
You burrow, you tunnel—you claw
through my locked doors.

You scream out of me—
Tears pierce me—break me—
Nothing but torrents of anguish
You chain me, you splinter me into pieces
of a broken weeping willow,
shattered like amber glass from a once beautiful flower vase.

Never A Fairytale
Princess

I was in a tower built for a princess, dark stones and emer-
    ald green ivy included
and the words, "I was no princess" fell on deaf ears

So I had to stay in the tower, perched on a windowsill
    watching the world like a bird on a wire
looking out at mountains and hills in the moonlight
    through dark wrought iron bars

designed to keep me in while looking beautiful in the way
    they curved, twirling in the air
like the blue moon dress I was forced to wear, since there's
    nothing else to wear in this tower.

All the while I was wishing for someone to climb the ivy
    of the tower instead of climbing on my hair—
it was not made of shining gold with the strength of the
    Goddess

I was not made to be climbed on; I was not made to be
    trapped in a sparkling layered dress; I was made to be
    taken from the tower and set free
to run and run and run

to fly like a witch on a broom,
Cackling at the freedom of flying over the moon

instead of being locked in a tower with parts of my hair
    falling out
as princes and princesses try to climb me instead of the
    ivy on the tower.

Painted in Place

inspired by "Alexandra, Princess of Wales" by Franz Xavier Winterhalter

* * *

The background was the color of the earth without gemstones
　　or gold because there was none to be had here
in this world of standing for hours, forced to be perfect in
　　place, scolded for a single hair or finger out of place
The dress was the color of the heavens after the fall of the an-
　　gels, dripping with the tears of those seraphim who could
　　no longer feel joy
as the princess could not weep with joy in her tight crown of
　　flowers
Trying to look beautiful so that the world can see the angel
　　instead of the pain and grief of being a princess
with the world on the other side of the frame that held the
　　princess in with paints mixed with her pain
So she could be stagnant, perfect in place

not a ruby red hair in disarray
blushing cheeks from fatigue and not from her womanly con-
    stitution
lips halted in the phrase, "Help me"
yet painted shut so no one could hear those two words
Black eyes empty of any love or light because being painted
    into a canvas as perfect as she was meant
Emptiness.

Unable to Fly

inspired by a "Bewitched" by Tina LeCour

* * *

My hat was dripping from the water that was thrown at me
while I stand alone in front of the stained glass amber moon
hands floating next to my side with no magick surrounding
 them to lovingly tickle my skin
there was no magick to be found in this world of suffocating
 hazy smoke

Obscuring the stars as if they were the mortal enemies to my
 witch spirit

a spirit that only wants to learn the magick of flight with the
 other witches
the ones who smile in their clear sky without the floating ash
 and staining soot
the witches who cackle in their pointed hats while I am
 grounded

Submerging in the waters of reflection that are filled with a
terrifying opaque whiteness

To fill my lungs and worm its way into my mind to make me
scream—till I bleed

The Ugly

I touch my face, the flaws etched into my skin
they capture me like electricity in a light bulb
I will get no pause from the photographers holding their cam-
eras

I touch the soul inside me, full of color and unfit for black
and white photos
The claws I see? The redness trickling down my body? My
own.
I'm ugly, down to the cracked ceramic bone.

Why am I this way? Unable to be captured on picture.
I can't keep the ugly at bay.
Can I change it the cracks, or the etches of scars?
Can I fit into a photo even with my little bit of color?
Or will the Beauty evade me?

(Untitled) That's Not Good Enough

Good:
To be desired or approved of.
—How does that feel?
—A word as unidentifiable as the stars in another galaxy cluster.

Enough:
As much as required.
—When am I enough?
—Is that enough?
—I'm tired (guess it is not enough).

Good enough : relationship
Being treated with respect, love, and affection.
—I carry a tissue box since one tissue is not enough
—Showers hide my tears when tissues cannot
—*silence*

nothing
i said
nothing
~~i'm fine. i'm fine.~~ I'm

Untitled I

Question 1: What is the correct way to say hello to a woman?
a) You look sexy standing there like that.
b) Do you have anything under those pants of yours? I have a bet going and I picked no.
c) You feel like going back to my place?
d) Don't say anything at all because it seems like men and women in my world have no manners and by not saying anything that proves this statement false.

Question 2: What is a good idea of a first date?
a) Going for a walk in the park while staring at other women nonstop.
b) Having coffee and paying no attention to me since your eyes are glued to your phone.
c) Going to lunch only to ask me to pay when the bill comes.
d) Saying we'll watch a movie when really all those hands feel like doing is feeling under my clothes even though I say, "No thank you."

Question 3: What is the correct way to say a woman looks good in her outfit?
a) You should put on makeup.
b) Why don't you try wearing tighter clothes?
c) Can you try doing something different with your hair?
d) None of the above.

Question 4: What is the right way to comfort a woman when she's bleeding so much she could strangle herself?
a) Saying that she should try being more active.
b) Telling her to go take a shower.
c) Saying that she should get on her knees for you.
d) Anything else besides the above that actually shows you care.

Question 5: What is a woman to do when she doesn't want to be alone but every man she finds leaves her angrier than before?
a)
b)
c)
d)

Someone Else Try to Fathom This

I don't apologize for the bluntness...

* * *

Things I didn't think I was going to hear:

A wave of curses because I refused to get into bed with you.
was it really hard to accept my no because there was blood
    pouring out of my cervix?
was it really hard to accept that I just didn't want to?
was it really hard to fathom the idea of enjoying one another
    without the heady throes of bodies

A bribery of doing your homework so that I could stay in
    your apartment because I thought I might like to spend
    time with you.

and that was the only thing that appealed to you about me?
the only thing that would let me stay?
were you really unable to thing of a movie or show we could
    binge together? a game we could play? i could go on

A constant string of excuses as to why we couldn't even go
    out for coffee and a walk in the park.
am I that hard to talk to?
am I that hard to remain serenely silent with?
are the only reasons to see me in three or four letters—sex,
    cunt, oral, anal, cry, sigh, tear, sigh

Months of ghosting before you text me to hook up. I said no.
was it really hard to try to be more than just a rake from Vic-
    torian England
because I'm not a whore, otherwise I would be paid
and even then you would find me cheap, so it wouldn't be
    worth, would it?

And someone tried to tell me that my true love would come
I just had to put myself out there...
Now I'm stuck in Groundhog Day.
Again.

Words Written in the Ink from My Body

You broke my mirror
with your sickly sweet words
that I didn't know would poison my eyes,
causing stinging, crackling pain
every time I cry thunderstorms
that crack and quake the infrastructure of my body.

You shattered my heart, as fragile as it already was,
with your lustful, willful gaze
My bed used to ring with the sound of peaceful joy
Now, all it does is drip
drip my tears into puddles.

All because you said you wished for me—
don't forget to add, "in bed."
Everything else—
Anything else—

"I don't have time"
was playing broken on my playlist,
the sad song becoming as meaningless as uncapitalized, end-
    less lines, all blurring together each time it's repeated.
(I've lost count)

All you said was, "I want you"
You keep forgetting to add, "in bed."
I would add it for you afterwards,
again and again.
each time I did another bloody slash would appear
on my broken mirror,
with the dust from my heart—a thief took it, I forgot to say.

with tears straining my face black and blue.

All I wanted was someone to love me,
to hold my fragile heart carefully,
to care about its little imperfections
all the chips, the cracks
All I wanted was someone to whisper, "I love you, I want
    you."
Not to forget to add, "in bed, bare as the moon."
it was written in the ink from my veins.

Why Can't I Leave?

Halting on the steps of a world that did nothing except hurt
   me—burn me—torment me—
was not an option

Being pushed when I would rather fight, rather climb, rather
   swim
was something I had no say in

My words were pushed from my mouth, a string of beads
   taken
without my consent

Those sparkling pale green and dark ribbon red pearls twist
   and twine their way around my wrists
forming restraints around all the wonders of my world

till there was nothing left, nothing shining
in this shadowed, inky black terrorizing world.

Reasons to Delete Hinge

—made with the help from a friend

* * *

1. It advertises love like a home-made chocolate cake, except it was a box cake instead.
2. The people you meet are about as sweet as the sugar in the dark chocolate icing
3. "Oh, yeah, I'm on here but I'm not looking for love, just friends with benefits" —and did anything I just said suggest that I am?
4. "You're hot, want to hookup?" —*taps [insert snarky and disgusted response] faster than I can bleach the words from my memory*
5. "How do you justify liking girls and guys, it's against the Bible" —How do you justify asking that question to someone you don't even know? I'm not living in medieval times

where divorce is punishable by excommunication—oh, wait... never mind.

6. The dates were packaged like store bought chocolate where I lower my expectations as I continue to take each bite because at the center the disappointment becomes overwhelming.

7. Hinge is no better than any dating app. A boxed cake hiding behind a photo, all done up with the prettiest icing from a can. But it will always be a boxed bake at its core.

Untitled II

This relationship was supposed to be for two
except there's only me, and then you
leaving me to blow away in the cold, crispy night
Straight into the back of a hard tree dripping with green
    moss and made of yew
leaving me to rot, stuck to the tree for so long that I devel-
    oped mildew
Growing, and growing, and growing, until it became worse
    than sickness—it became a blight
built to destroy civilizations and children, like ash and soot
    in a flue
Dark and lingering, unwavering in its stains on the skin, that
    much is true

Only one thing is worse than previously unblemished soot-
    stained skin
and that was you—a man in sharkskin—
You who decided that only your desires mattered
while you gnashed your teeth on my too-thin skin

wet from the slick dew that layered my sickly white sins
of which there was only one: trying to love, only to be left
    battered

Laying against a tree that was now only green, with spots of
    white pigmentation
dark green vines that used to be filled with warm blood, now
    running cold
even though the world was spinning faster than the colors of
    fire
the tree stood
where I was thrown against it, laying... endlessly

Labours

Three... two... one

Stop hounding me about my orchard
or else I'll find a rope to hang myself on
dangling from my moss covered branches
Pomegranates falling on the tear-glistening green grass
like one, two, three

Stop berating me over the spilt water
as if it was my fault you tipped the glass
The water spreading to the other end of my table
twinkling in the light of the beeswax candles I anointed my-
    self
to try to please you

There are no apologies for the words that come out of my
    mouth now:
"What other labours will you make me do?"
"What other problems are my fault?"

"Do you think I enjoy the silence in our bedchamber?"
"I don't think it would be a bad idea for our love to end.
It's already as dead as a rotting rose anyways."

There are no apologies for the words I call you:
Domineering and sexist
As poisonous as nightshade
As beautiful as a wart
Callous, a scar that I failed to avoid
Harrowing—the villain without a chance of redemption

There are no apologies for the dreams I want (not with you):
Smiles and laughter
Walks in the park
Coffee together, sharing a berry tart
A bedchamber filled with talking
An understanding that cannot be put into words

I apologize for none of it.

Kill Me, Heart, Before I Break

Can I ask
to be killed
before I break
Heart, please—kill
me, and my
terribly bruised soul

I just thought
to ask that
so the bruises
don't turn into
festering infected wounds
to leech life

I feel it
in the air
like terrifying electricity

about to be
crying with sparks
filling the world

Don't tell me
to be patient
to have hope
to try more
to keep dreaming
to keep singing

There are no
songs to sing
dreams to keep
tries to have
hope for more
patience to weather

No more. Please.
Kill me Heart
Please, kill me.
Before I break—
Please, kill me.
—Beyond all repair.

See It Now?

Care to fill my mouth with something other than your mem-
     ber?
Care to fill it with talks and laughter?

Want to hold me softly, without bruising me?
Want to caress my skin that is spotless of purple hues?

Dream of something more than the sound of sex?
Dream of spending time outside in the world?

I do.
I do, nonstop.

This is no longer what I care for
this abuse of my heart, unable to feel joy.

I stare at my skin and discard the sights of yellow-green heal-
     ing bruises
mixed with the fresh blue-purples, a hideous sight.

I daydream during my hours at work of an apartment to
    share with a heart
to match my own in passion and love—

and that was not ever you.
No, it was never going to be you...

A Plate Full of Bitter Doubts

1. Finding a warm set of arms to call home
2. Being able to be kissed so passionately (by black painted lips) that I burn
3. Sharing a bag of popcorn on my living room couch while wearing his sweater
4. Being able to say three little words with the nervousness of a seven year old about to jump in the pool's deep end
5. Laughing till I'm crying because of something they said
6. Being on a date that doesn't involve a bedroom and only ends in cuddles and chocolate
7. Coming home to a smile of softness on her face
8. Crying because I said something terrible and yet they forgave me anyway
9. Being upset with him because he forgot about our plans, but grumbling as I sit in his embrace—even when I'm mad I can't stay away; it's love
10. Staying in bed for hours, just talking to them

11. Finding love in a place where college is just another word for adult elementary school

Can This Truly Be How the Story Ends?

When did I say you could hold my heart in your greasy hands
so you could twist it into a misshapen piece of flesh

When did I say you could pull the ends of my heart with your
    dirt-filled fingernails
so you could pierce it with your poison, hurting me on every
    level imaginable

levels I didn't even know where possible, didn't know even
    existed
until you decided you could lay claim to my heart, like every
    other defiler in every other storybook

with a princess or queen that the man demanded to own, to
    keep, to hold tightly
until the woman was dead—no longer a princess or queen

no longer her own
No longer

an ending no woman wants to see.

Finding Him...

Words I Can Say Instead

Good morning, handsome (And I don't mean that as a joke)
How are you? (I hope you didn't get COVID again)
Are you okay? (Please be okay)
You're really smart (and I want to talk to you all day)
Please be careful (that's my heart you seem to be holding)
Where you been? (I've missed you too much to say)
How is life? (without me being with you)
You inspire me (to want more, with you)
I had fun (just spending time with you)
Wanna watch Disney? (Just us? Please say yes.)
I'm really happy (only with you)
Thanks for everything (For listening to me, for letting me
    hear your voice)
My favorite person (who I can't imagine being without)

Fools and Warriors

Romeo and Juliet were fools amongst a court of jesters, with
    bells swinging from their inane and empty heads
whereas my head is filled with a strength that rivals the im-
    mortal and all-powerful gods
I fight the foes stronger than mortal humans carrying swords
    and shields: Distance, Loneliness, and Dreams.

I fight stronger, faster, and more often, never allowing myself
    to fail
to yield to a force so impure, so vile, that it makes weaker
    men and women shiver
wishing for peace despite standing in the middle of a blood-
    ied battleground with scattered and decaying limbs

In the distance, I see the Three smiling at me, drawing near
with feathered helmets and scratched helms glinting in the
    light
no sweat on their bodies as there is on mine

Distance likes to laugh in my face, walking hand in hand with
   Loneliness.
Their beauty is as great as their icy prickling cruelty, con-
   stantly prodding me till I am red from head to toe
before Dreams decides to take me in my unwaking moments
   to flaunt your face, your smile, and your laughter
telling me that I cannot have you, because you are not mine...

No matter how hard I fight, no matter how hard I jump to
   the side—
arms aching, legs shaking, sweat flying into the air like sharp
   invisible arrows—
breathe coming out in short bursts again—and—again and...
   again
all I can do is prolong it—
The End

I Do It Better Than Tinkerbell

I collect little found objects that catch my eye.
Dirt covered coins, little acorns that have fallen from
  branches, a bit of glass here and there

all pale in comparison to the finding of you,
taken by someone else yet somehow catching my eyes.

I try to pinpoint the why—why I need you
All I can think of is the way your voice sounds, sending flut-
  ters of rhythm into me

or the way your brown eyes turn caramel with light and joy
as we discuss the intricacies of Nintendo versus Playstation

or maybe it could be the way we discuss how the last three
  movies of Star Wars don't exist
after wondering if we could make a Jabba the Hutt costume

Do I have to even tell you how much I want to be the Lady to
    your Lord,
gifting you with a sword to cut down the things in our
    path—people too.

It runs that deep, because I found my eyes catching on your
    every crack and crevice
peering into the darkness of the shadows to know it all

You are the best treasure I have found in my life
worth it all and still completely priceless, forever and always.

Untitled III

There were words in my mind that I could not say to you:
1. I really like you—like really like you
2. I wish you weren't dating someone who makes you so unhappy you cry
3. I want to stop asking you for advice with my boyfriends and come to you so I can smile instead, because you make me smile even when the world is falling
4. I stay up late to talk to you because I want to know how you have been, because I love the sound of your voice
5. I call you during your work shifts because I want to see your face
6. I say we are just friends because I can't bear the thought of losing you, even though you suspect my feelings
7. I love that you text me even though you know I'm asleep—it means that you care about me
8. You can tell me anything and I will listen, because I really, really like you
9. I don't think I can help my feelings much longer
10. I want to be your girlfriend

Untitled IV

You were with someone who didn't see you
someone who was as venomous as the world-eating serpent
as beautiful as the pale green scales glinting in the light as it
    moves

I told you that I really liked you
because love was not something I could say, not yet, not be-
    fore daybreak
but at least my soul was not as spiteful or vengeful as the
    Ouroboros

You could not believe the words that poured from my mouth
As if it were the golden tears from Freyja's eyes.
I had to say them, I had to release them from the caverns of
    my heart.

You travelled far and wide, from the heavens to the earths,
    north to east, west to south

to find the reason behind my words, to find the "insanity" in
   my mind turning counterclockwise.
I held the map to the treasure in my hand, waiting for you to
   hand over the starchart, so we could share hearts.

I would continue to wait eternity after eternity
as Odin did when he was hung from the mighty moss-covered
   branches of the World Tree
because you are *my* magick.

I'm in a Taylor Swift Song

You make me think of Taylor Swift songs
watching someone else walk down the aisle
A hideous dress to match her hideous heart

Watching as she took my place beside you
waiting to finally speak out and say,
"Don't make me wait any longer. Can you feel my love?

Don't you know that I've loved you
for a while now
I have loved you

for longer than I can say,
in every reality I have loved you.
Do you need me to say it again?"

You make me think of Taylor Swift songs

of finding an enchanting dance in a ballroom filled with
    faerie lights
and me dancing my way home

alone.
Until you knock on my door from 4,349 miles away
and say

"I am so lucky to have met you.
Would you care to continue
this dance?"

Then I smiled, feeling the enchantment strengthen
taking your hand in mine, to step out in the midst of fireflies
baby blue and ivory dress swishing

to continue our dance
that was not a waltz
but a play at who could enchant who.

You make me think of Taylor Swift songs
as I watch the sparks fly from the space between us
even if someone else would call them pixels on a screen

and yet you were still not wholly mine
because you had her
but she didn't make sparks fly

Not like we could,
as we watched Disney movies of family talents or alien fugi-
    tive ships crashing
Talking for hours afterwards, making sparks twist and twirl
    into dances of their own

sparks flying between the lips of you and I
making me wonder what it would be like if those lips were
    mine
if those sparks could be said aloud, to show the connection
    between us

A reckless thunderstorm would be able to describe me
as I continue to encroach on your life, unwilling to end the
    spray of electricity
Those apprehensive thoughts won't end those bright blue
    sparks—no, never.

You make me think of Taylor Swift songs
where chapter one of us hasn't even started
Even though I'm constantly button smashing the keyboard

trying to get the words on the page,
trying to get the clock to move forward
so that I can turn the pages

Pretending this is nothing, it's not working for me—for
    us—the keys fly in the air

Forcing me to get busy so that I can make money for a new
   keyboard
instead of fixing the keys on the one I broke

since broken things don't end up working in the end
and I need to push the buttons to start that chapter one.
Instead, I'm finishing with "The End,"

and scratching it out with a pen.
since there is no end for us,
especially since there isn't even a page one yet.

We haven't started yet,
like the Taylor Swift songs I play on repeat
imagining every possible way that could be us.

Telling a Story in Short

I've known from day one
that I'm wishful

I care so much
I want to know you

I'm not used to hearing what you say
even from the one who were supposed to hold my heart

I want to tell every day that I care
And sometimes is not enough

Days run by, words that tear at my very soul
It threatens the world around me

"You deserve more"
It puts me on the cusp of crying

"Come to me

I will change your mood for you"

You are perfect—words on the tip of my tongue
and I almost tell you that

"Did you have fun?
Tell me about your day"

Words that I never hear
Words that force me to fall

deeper and deeper in love
with you.

Untitled V

Emotionally depressed means that I get my phone to text you
furiously typing the letters to string together the words, "I
    need you."
in a way that doesn't come off as me winning "Third Wheel
    of the Century."

You being emotionally unavailable is my curse, something
    that needs a cursebreaker.
A man with a staff and long gray beard that puts Merlin's to
    shame
or someone with a bit more edge and eyeliner that makes
    Arthur look weak.

Someone to take care of the reasons why we can't be together,
To change my world as I've told I wish
as you've said you also dream of.

There's no imagination that can create a world without you
    and I;

A world where I don't see your name on my phone when I
    wake up
or for you to see my name when you do—

A world without you, without us, is no world at all
is a world where I refuse to exist
where there is nothing but terror and loneliness...

A world where no whisper of soulmates fly through constel-
    lations
where laughter does not ring a string of melodies
Where light does not exist.

The Wings and Song of a Meadowlark

Have you found my lost heart
that is now suddenly beating like a meadowlark
free in the wind, becoming undone by your voice
as if I had any other choice

Unraveled like a string from a tapestry of angelic colors
Hues of lightweight gold, shades of vibrant blues, better than
    all the summers
spent across time, with nothing to show for it, no one to
    spread those tawny wings
So I cherish the voice you bring, causing my lips to sing

The Song of the Meadowlark, adding a shimmer to my every-
    day
creating waters in the form of a bright cerulean blue bay
to whisk me away, to a world without the dark shivers of
    nothingness

creating a field or an aura of thick somethingness.

A field for my wings to beat, to fly, to nest within the bright
    caramel-colored wooden branches
Creating a song so loud that it could be heard in the moun-
    tains of another world, starting avalanches.
But my lips do not care one bit. For so long the only sound I
    made created tears, not music
And now, because of you finding my heart, because of your
    voice, there will be no other sounds besides a melody of
    notes.

You changed me, even before you knew how much I loved you
how much I became something new
Something that was decaying and translucent
Is now full of color and music, exploding with a soul too
    bright for anything except you.

Three More Letters Needed

I dared to tell you that I liked you as more than that six-let-
   tered word
I dared to let it be known while I was dying in the heat, mak-
   ing my head swim with tyrannical inhibition
I don't know what came over me in that moment—that
   turned into another moment—
and another.
Until I couldn't stop repeating it
couldn't stop telling you the ways I would show you how
   much I could love you
how much I dreamt of you and I holding hands and being as
   close as we could possibly be
no air molecules between us to hold us apart.
I dared to tell you it all, and I do not regret
one
single
part.

I like you more than six letters
I like you in a way that creates a nine-lettered word.

Untitled VI

We were together before we knew how to say it out loud. With the air feeling our unsaid words, with the distance between us knowing to pull us together. We saw it in each other's eyes, in the way you were the first one I called when I woke up, and I was the last person you called before you went to sleep. We knew it in the moments where we thought of one another in the little things that would make time shine with euphoria. Like watching Star Wars movies with each other while eating Wookie Cookies and Yoda Sodas. We were the definition of "together but not." And we didn't know how to say it out loud. Would time ring the unsaid words? Would the distance close?

Would I finally tell you... that I liked you more and more each day... that it was enough to love you?

Surrounded by Comforting Love

My favorite sweater is not a brand new sweater but one that
   is worn and patched
showing the way it was loved and hurt, and healed
It is the way it feels too big from being worn instead of tight
   like something new
It is the way some areas are patchier than others because the
   blue yarn has been worn down and darned over time
It only makes you more aware of the details from the fuzzy
   warm fabric

Why settle for a new sweater with no wear and tear, no love,
   and no character
when a perfectly good patched and unique sweater is waiting
   in the closet?
A sweater that no one else has or will ever have because it be-
   longs to no one else
With details that only one person can know

My favorite sweater fits me and only me, with more wear and
   tears that only I can give it, to show that I love it.

My sweater may not know it yet, may not want to think
   about it,
but I do love it. I will always love the way it feels even if it
   thinks itself ugly.
If my sweater gives me the time of day to point out all the
   ways I know it
I will do it, again and again and again—forever—
My favorite sweater is not something new or perfect; my fa-
   vorite sweater is perfectly imperfect.

Loving Him...

Trigger Warnings:
Sex
Depression

You Are All

You don't see
How beautiful, *how beautiful*
You are.
You don't see your worth—
You're worth it,
Worth more than a gem hewn from sunlight
by dwarves eagerly trying to dig through a mountain of dark-
    ness to get to its pure starlight power
and you are worth of all of that
and more.
Showing you your beauty—your worth
are the best days of my life.

7/27/2022

The stars reach for the blue night sky
as I reach for you.
The moon chases the sun
as I chase after you.
All are choices, all are actions,
actions that speak of a love greater than time.
The stars love the enchanting sky
The moon loves the sun
And I love you.

Untitled VII

We go together like chocolate and sea salt,
only we are smoother than the sand that was caressed by the
    cresses of the ocean
because we knew when to give and when to say enough.

So many didn't know the difference between giving and be-
    ing taken
for everything they were and were going to be,
becoming something akin to the trenches of a lost war.

We cannot save them, only show them that there is some-
    thing out there for them.
A cozy day with a hot cup of cocoa where we dip our own
    halves of chocolate inside
swirl it about, and look up at each other as we feel the choco-
    late melt in our mouths.

How To Say "I Love You"

1. I miss you
2. Are you up?
3. Are you leaving?
4. You're a dork
5. Come over here
6. Come snuggle me
7. Don't leave me
8. Please, don't leave
9. Jeg savner dig (I'll miss you)

Untitled VIII

I cried in your arms
mountains of little dewdrops spilling across your shoulders
    and arms
I cried to you
"Don't make me go, don't let me go"
You held me tightly
embracing my night with the feelings of unshakable earth
I sobbed
"Don't make me go, don't let me go, it's too long, it's too far"
I couldn't get air
even though I was the night incarnate, surrounded by it
That's what it did to me.
"Let me stay.
Make me stay.
I can't survive without you."
I can't get air.
"I'm untethered without the feeling of you."
I can't get air.

7/30/2022

When the night is dark,
with no stars present

all I can think of is
Where are you?

When the stars are full of bliss
it's you.

When the sun is shining
it's you.

When a smile hits my face
like a rocket to the stars
it's you.

Every moment, every smile, every bliss, every shine
is you.

7/31/2022

Luck exists in the number three
It shows up in the form of a found penny
It likes to travel in the shades of green
and Luck grows on Mother Earth as a four leafed clover

I had none of these
Not the number three
Not a penny lost and now found
Not a speck of green even in a four leafed clover to save my
    life

I had nothing to wish upon
Yet somehow I was lucky
because I found you
amongst the ivy green covered stones of my wishing well

I fell in love with you,
I said the words,
"I love you

Always

Forever
Till the end of time
And beyond."
And then you said to me, sweetly and beautifully...

"I love you too."
And I smiled, knowing,
I had luck kissing me somewhere.

Existing in Time

I stare at a ceiling while you hum and sing off-key
yet strike the right keys in my mind
To tell it these wonderful, beautiful, perfect words:
"Shut the fuck up and let my girlfriend exist in peace!"

It works, creating a blanket of peace that I had never known
    before you.
The keys keep playing dutifully as you hum, allowing my eyes
    to close
seeing only the serene blackness of the universe without an-
    other breathing soul near—
you do not really count since you are nothing but pixels in a
    screen and half my soul.

You snuggle me with your voice, an atmosphere befitting
    Morpheus being woven like a tapestry of dreams and bliss
                little threads being woven to create the
                    rusted hands of time Themself,
all the while I never notice the movement

as the world spins on
and on.

8/7/2022

Over four thousand two hundred and fifty miles from me to
    you
Over six hours a day do we sometimes talk
Over five thousand words do we thumb into our phones for
    each other.
We ache—
We cry—for each other.
Our wet eyes long for the sight
of each other.
We are two souls pulled apart by
more than four thousand two hundred and fifty miles.
Born on opposite ends of the world,
we found each other!
Land and water, bitter and terrible,
they cannot hold us apart!
We yearn—
We dream—
We seek—
We *crave*—

each other.
One day, one day we will be together
forever.
always.
past the end of time.
And then we will shake the world with our love.

8/8/2022

You are my light.
You are my knight.
You are my king.
You are the person I cling to, a song I praise.
You are my whole world...
a love that has unfurled like golden-sparkling white wings...
I did not think that someone could sprout a love
so deep, so full, that it sprouted the wings of an angel.
What I could not feel,
believed I could not feel,
you made me feel.
You made me feel true love.

The Color of Doom and Gloom

Sitting in my room I feel a sense of precarious stagnation in my soul. You are no longer pixels on my screen so the world feels like the color of spilt ink: black, thick, and unavoidable. It covers my hands and drips up my arms and onto my legs, spreading until not even the pale pallor of my skin can be seen. I'm the dark side of life without you, the place no one wants to be and everyone fears: melancholic misery. So tied to you am I that when I can't see you, speak with you, all I do is sit... and wait... in my room that makes cavern-dwelling goblins balk.

8/9/2022

I read poetry about long distance relationships. I think about the miles that keep us apart... only four thousand three hundred and forty-nine miles from me to you—*only*, I laugh in my head. I thought to myself that I cannot wait for the day that the distance between us is zero. I cannot wait for the day when you are holding me and I am being held by you. I cannot wait for the days when I wake up and have you next to me; the days when I sleep and you reach across the bed to find my body. There is so much to look forward to that the miles don't matter and I know that all that matters is when I reach for the sky to finally be with you forever, the number of miles will get smaller and smaller until they reach zero.

You Seem to Need a List...

1. You talk to me, for hours, about the nonsense and the nonsensical—there's a difference for us.
2. You tell me you want me for more than sex—and it made me cry, even if I have heard it time and time again.
3. Makeup or not, sexy fishnets or pajamas, I am beautiful to you—something I've never had.
4. No one has made me relaxed as you do.
5. With you I am wanted and loved. We talk about Decembers, about how we will spend our days hugging, snuggling, cuddling, kissing... and I can't wait... I can't let go of the yearning I feel for it—for you.
6. When I am scared I always come to you.
7. The universe pushed us together against all odds, my heart and soul. Countless odds vanished the moment I fell for you and you for me. The amount of card readings I've done is numberless, and they all say love, happiness, and good fortune. The universe has spoken, we are meant to

be—it's in the stars, it's in the whispers of the moon and the shine of the sun. We are meant to be.

My eyes look at you and see love.
Du er alt og mere. (You are all and more.)

9/6/2022

Some days I burst at the thought of
seeing you
hearing you
talking with you.
And some days
I want to cry for hours because
seeing you
hearing you
talking with you
reminds me that I can't
I can't touch you
smell you
lay next to you.
And then I want to sob
I think
Four thousand three hundred and forty-nine miles—
Too far.
Today, is a day
and I want to cry.

I want to cry and cry
I cannot be with you
the world is too big and we are on its poles
alone.

There is Nothing More Than This

My hands run through your hair
while you looked down and stared

with those perfect chocolate eyes
that complemented my sea-deep hazel ones.

I don't have to say,
"Let your hands run over my skin,"
"Kiss me till I bleed"

because you do that already.
Our minds are too far gone in our soul-link.

I sigh, your hands reaching
to caress
every inch of skin—that goes pink

with ecstasy and lecherous eroticism
And there's no need to call for an exorcism

because I was <u>born</u> a demon,
like you,
and we owned it

on the day we met each other
and decided that we could unleash it
to let ourselves <u>burn</u>

while we stared at each other
letting our bodies run naked
as your teeth gnashed on my skin
and my teeth pierced your skin.

Our glistening skin collides once more,
making sparks fly

like the lyrics in a Taylor Swift song
except the time has elapsed past four minutes and thirty-one
    seconds.

and went straight to 00:00
because when you and I are together

time breaks
with how we break each other

while we smile.

Slick skin desperate for ice
to cool the perpetual heat

Dangerous eyes always gleaming
daring for more.

Chapped and aching lips
from the kissing, the biting, the nipping

and as soon as we stop, breathe, and close our eyes
the clock starts back up, and it is 00:01.

. . . .
then we see each other, our breaths having become stable one
    more
now turn unstable
and the clock—time—breaks

it's 00:00
and I'm on top of you, growling as I devour your skin again.

9/20/2022

You are my Moon and Stars,
The part of my days that I love most.
Without you the world seems Bleak and Lifeless,
Cold and Void of Light.
You are the one thing that gets me through my days,
the part of my days that I seek more than anything else.
I care for nothing else,
as I look for Your Shine in the night sky.

9/24/2022

I wish you could see the way the water runs over my pale red blotched skin. I wish you could feel the soap and bubbles that slowly glide down my smooth body. The way the water runs my hair smooth like silk—it yearns for your touch. My fingers run through my hair in place of yours, and they should be running over your skin and your hair. If only you were here, if only I could touch you and you me. If only we could breathe air in the same room filled with steam and falling clear droplets. If only...

Neverending

The threads of my hair are pulled in between my fingers while
    I stare agitated
at a language that may as well be alien—a series of insane and
    crackhead ramblings.
I try to make sense of it all but the letters just swirl around
    my cloudy vision
like the colorful cartoon unicorns from Deadpool's strangely
    mad hatter genius mind.
Trying to pull his thought process together is easier than
    looking at a language with too many diphthongs
too many non-rule rules, too many exceptions and "just know
    it" statements for me to comprehend.
It's all mashed into mush—
and I do it all for you, because it is only fair that I learn your
    language as you have learned mine

Even if it is the ramblings of a madman from space I will
    learn it
I will breathe it

I will write in it, in more than just a few phrases
I will write love letters to you in your language
I will create works of art in this unstructured language for the
    world to see the depths of my love
only to see that there is no end, no bottom, only
a beginning, a birth, and a growth
only more and more endless
love

9/27/2022

Jeg elsker dig, altid. (I love you, always.)
Jeg savner dig, altid. (I miss you, always.)
Jeg vil have dig, altid. (I want you, always.)
Og kun dig altid—for evigt. (And only you always—forever.)
Du er min elskede, min, og kun min og kun min elskede, al-
    tid—for evigt. (You are my love, mine, and only my love,
    always—forever.)
Don't forget, ved det altid. (I know it always.) You will never
    lose me, du har mig (you have me), you will always have
    me. Because I love you, altid og for evigt. (always and for-
    ever.)

10/8/2022

You are my greatest and only real love. You make me sane. And you make me smile when I need to. You tell me when I'm wrong and you say it's okay. I could go on and on and give you pages of why you are my greatest and only real love and by the end you would be in tears and so would I and would we be holding each other if we were in the same room, so I'll just leave it here.

My Port in the Storm

I look at a rainbow with no color. Not a spec of red, not an ounce of orange... not even a sliver of violet to break the shades of gray. It reminds me of the way I feel when I am without you and your warm touch to light my way. Color-less, devoid of the shimmering they bring in the light. Like diamonds dancing in the sky. Except all that is here is a gray bleakness that is my home. An emptiness that I shiver in fear of. It came suddenly, too, with no warning. Like a freak storm blowing the trees down. Except now, it was blowing me down. The only port I can see safety in... is you.

10/24/2022

You are my Light.
You make me smile when there is nothing to smile about,
when the day has gone gray and no Color deems themselves
    fit to enter.
You are my Dark.
You make me into your siren of the deep, singing to summon
    the rain for the drought.
You turn into my own siren, your voice carrying with mine in
    a sinful tenor.
I made you mine.
You made me yours.
We are Blue,
Sea and Sky,
You—I—
Inseparable.

You

The moments

the moments when I watch the colors on the screen
I feel this emptiness
taking root
building empires
inside of me,
turning me over, again and again, in an endless wave of noth-
   ingness.

That is a moment

where I cry

for you.

because I want you.

The moments

when I mull over poetry, brave my way over prose,
smile and laugh, over ingenious plot points,
feel the warmth come into my heart

I stop.

and realize

you aren't here
to hold me
to whisper sweet words into my ear

That is a moment

where I cry,

for you.

because I want you.

The moments

when I feel everything too much—too fast—can't breathe!

and you are there but
instead of your warm flushed skin with coursing blood
there are pixels of cold heartless—nothingness

That is a moment—

I cry.

for you.

because I want you.

and I know—I know
it is not your fault but
you aren't here

I love you

and you aren't here

You aren't here

The moments create a moment—
the one thing I want—

your warmth caressing me with your love,
your whispers telling me you love me—
is not here—

you are not here

A moment where I cry.

12/28/2022

The sun shines but I feel no warmth
The light is bright but it is dark out—that never bothered me
    before
My eyes without the sight of you are sore
My hands without the feel of you are cold
All I want is to feel you
All my eyes yearn for is your face, your eyes
I just want you
but life is cruel
and the distance is even crueler.
When neither are our enemies all we will have are smiles and
    laughter.

Untitled VIII

i love you more than five words. how could five words ever express my love? how can eight words do the same, when the depth is so much greater? i love you more than fourteen words because you are my waystation in the darkness. a waystation that protects me from the evils in the world i walk in and the world i dream in. these nightmares are meant to feed on my fear and anxiety, my anger and hate, till you hold me and become a beacon of light to chase them away. so, how can five words or eight words or even fourteen words ever express how much i love you even when i struggle against the light because the nightmare monsters can be too much.

Polaroids in Time

8/11/2022
I start my days when yours is a few hours from over. You start yours when mine are ending. I stay up late so that I can call you and ask you to stay on the line with me till I sleep. When I do I sleep all the better for it, with cool clear night skies and soft twinkling stars. Dreams fill me, rather than twisting nightmares of bile and venom—black worms filling every part of my body. I will wait up late for you every night until finally our days and nights are the same, until you sleep in the same bed as I do. My sleep will then always be filled with bliss—beautifully, glistening, from the heavens— every single one.

* * *

9/21/2022
I can't think—
The white and indigo lilies in my garden do nothing
to bend my mind to soothing breaths
No in, no out, no in, no out—

no—

Outside, I'm being chased by wardens—everyday

I can't feel—feel too much—waves in my body, pushing and
    pulling—endlessly

My poetry does little make me feel—not feel

No more poetry, I'm cornered—

I can't—breathe—

The colors of the sky—at night—do nothing—to give
    me—breath

Wardens have me caged—

there are no more colors in this world.

But You come to break my barbed cage

the lack of Thought

the lack of Feeling—too much Feeling—push and pull

the lack of Breath

All that I want

All that I need

Comes from You.

Tiy are the Key to my World—

Hope—

Life—

Meaning—

You give me

Everything.

* * *

4/18/2023

Ups
We smile. We laugh. We dream. And the light never dims. Everything is encapsulated in euphoria, crystals glimmering in the space around you—around us. Mountains move in your brown eyes while stars shoot across mine. Petals shimmer in your skin, turning rosy. Mine shimmer with crystalline oceans. When our laughter creates tears in our eyes, you create rivers befitting Egypt.

Downs
We both have a hard time keeping the smiles on our faces. I say to you, "We don't have to smile. We can just be. Together." You nod, I nod. We just are. Together. On the bed. Alone. And we find solace in each other's arms. Silence was the third wheel to our togetherness. We didn't mind one bit.

Ups
The sun shone even in the swirling chocolate of your eyes—my favorite sweet. Your touch was better than a cloud's, and it was all I wanted. We learned to smile again. We learned to laugh our hearts out, till they ached! We danced, we loved, and we loved each other—always. There was no end. There will never be an end

Downs
Storms hit—not outside—Inside. We still hold Love in our interlaced hands. Because there was no end
You said to me, "Is it alright if I am not smiling or happy? Or feel like talking?" I laughed, bittersweetly, "I don't feel like

talking either. So yeah, it's fine. So long as I don't have to talk too." You took my hand, the coldness making me shiver with recognition. You pulled me onto our bed. We stayed there, silently, watching whatever we wanted on the tv.

Ups and Downs
They have one thing in common. We are together through it all. Even when we aren't smiling—we are together—always. There's no end

I Have Another Love Letter For You

You are my other half, the part of me I always needed and never knew where to find to become whole again. I wished we lived closer so I could show you every day how much I love you, how much I miss you. You are the king in my kingdom, the soul that I was missing. I cannot possibly express how much I can't wait to move to Denmark and live with you forever. You are my favorite person, the one I can't live without. I love you always and I never ever want to lose you or what we have... Baby, you are the love of my life. You have shown me what love is, which was something I never knew before. I can't begin to thank you for that. I love you so much...

For Him

When all is said and done, I have to say—
words, that's all I know—
you are my lifeline (the rest are in pieces around me)
the only one I can cling to today
While all the wolves gnash their venom-filled fangs—
serrated so when they pull out to bite me again it rips
my blemished skin to red, red ribbons—

One glittering gold band amidst the red, red ribbons
my lifeline
You are the shine of the moon
                the gleam of the stars
                                the only one who will my lips curl

a smile—a rarity in this day

All the time of the day slips away
I have no care

He cares for me, because of it
i cling to Him for it
i know if my hands slip,
       i slip

            away.

one glittering gold band amidst the sea of red, red ribbons.

Destined

I have made so many poems
encompassing all the ways, all the words, all the touches, all
   the smells...
that come from Us.
There was no way that I could weave together words to create
the essence of Us
the soul of Us
in even a hundred poems.

We were more than the sands of the bottomless oceans
we were more than all the stars in the sky, forming the cradle
   of the universe
more than seeds in the earth, coming from ancestors of over
   a millenia ago.
We were more than all of it combined.
To create a hundred poems wouldn't even cover a speck of Us
and those who did not understand, did not know how much
   of Us there was
could not fathom the meaning of Us.

All we could do was hope that our story would be written in
the Sands of Time
spoken of between the Stars of Galaxies in the endless sky
seen in dancing Elder Trees that bend and weave throughout
the earth

For we knew how glorious it was, and so, too, should the Universe.

Alexandria Green is a poet and aspiring author. She works nonstop on her stories and poems, often having to quickly type them out in her notes app on her phone. Her mind constantly crafts things that refuses to leave her until it's written out. While Alexandria loves poetry, her favorite poet being Emily Dickinson, she hopes that her next published work will be one of her novels.

If asked, Alexandria will say that the reason that she didn't go with a publishing house was because she didn't want the writes of her works to be given up. She wanted complete control with no contracts to take that away, which is why she paid for her own ISBNs. She also didn't like that so many places didn't want authors and poets to submit their works elsewhere and how they were forced to wait years sometimes to know if it got accepted or not.

When she isn't writing and being an absolute loot goblin on Baldur's Gate 3 or Divinity Original Sin 2, Alexandria can be found reading in her basement, watching a show about DC Comics or Marvel heroes, or at her local zoo watching the otters play around.